The man who rediscovered America

Other biographies by John Upton Terrell

The man who rediscovered America

A BIOGRAPHY

OF JOHN WESLEY POWELL

by John Upton Terrell

WEYBRIGHT AND TALLEY
New York

The man who rediscovered America

I IN THE LATE SPRING OF 1878, ONE OF THE most significant, remarkable, and controversial books ever written by an American was published in Washington, D.C. Its author was John Wesley Powell, geologist in charge of the United States Geographical and Geological Survey of the Rocky Mountain Region. His title, although lengthy, did not suggest other impressive credentials that might have been used to identify him. He had a distinguished Civil War record as a major of artillery on the staff of General Ulysses S. Grant. His right hand and forearm, shattered by a minnie ball at Shiloh, had been amputated. After the war he had won fame as an explorer. He had led a small group of daring men in a descent of the Green and Colorado Rivers through a vast region that was designated UNKNOWN on the maps of western America. Distinguished as a geologist and ethnologist, he stood in the foremost rank of American scientists.

1]

John Wesley Powell called his small book—it contained less than 200 pages—*Report on the Lands of the Arid Region of the United States*. Inserted in the text were the drafts of two legislative measures that advocated drastic revisions in Federal statutes governing the settlement and development of the Western public domain. Indeed, the bills proffered radical departures from existing practices that would have given the Federal government full control of new Western water and grazing projects.

In accordance with required procedures, Powell had submitted his manuscript first to J. A. Williamson, Commissioner of the General Land Office. Williamson had sent it on the same day to Carl Schurz, Secretary of the Interior, his and Powell's superior. He had not, Williamson wrote Schurz, had time to study the report or the bills, but he felt they were of "great importance" and that Powell's views, whatever they might be, were "entitled to great weight."

Within twenty-four hours, Secretary Schurz not only had found time to read the report but had sent it to Samuel J. Randall, Speaker of the House of Representatives, with an enthusiastic letter of endorsement. "In view of the importance of rendering the vast extent of [western] country referred to available for agricultural and grazing purposes, I have the honor to commend the views set forth by Major Powell and the bills submitted herewith to the consideration of Congress."

It is hardly possible that Speaker Randall troubled to do more than glance at Schurz's letter, if he saw it at all, for on the day it came into his office it and the Powell report were referred to the Committee on Appropriations, through which they would pass to the Government Printing Office. Randall, however, would soon become familiar with *Arid Lands*, as the Major's book would be dubbed, for he and

2]

every other member of Congress would be involved in the disturbance it generated.

Only 1800 copies of *Arid Lands* were issued. Soon after they were distributed to personages of the official government family—cabinet members, committee chairmen, and Western senators and representatives—Washington lazed in the summer doldrums. Capitol Hill was all but deserted, and only in the Executive Branch did Federal workers suffer out the humidity created by the odorous swamps along the Potomac. Anyone who had means of escape vanished from the scene.

Obviously, the Appropriations Committee in ordering such a small number of *Arid Lands* printed had not thought it would attract much attention or have a great demand. Actually, not all 1800 copies had been distributed. Some were held in the Printing Office stockroom, but, under the rules, they could be released only on order of a member of Congress. Powell himself had difficulty obtaining eight copies which he wished to send to his friend Professor Othniel C. Marsh, the noted Yale paleontologist and president of the National Academy of Sciences.

As the year 1879 began, and new appropriations bills were being written, it became apparent that a turmoil over *Arid Lands* was in the making. John Wesley Powell, always highly respected as a scientist, had suddenly become a political force who could not be ignored. Moreover, his supporters, although comparatively few, were becoming increasingly vocal. Adoption of his land-reform recommendations, as outlined in *Arid Lands,* was being urged by several representatives who had for some time been striving to halt the corruption, extravagance, and wastefulness being tolerated, if not abetted, by the Congress under the deceitful excuse of contributing to the development of Western resources. The National Academy had let it be known that its members strongly favored Powell's proposals. On the other hand, cries of alarm were heard from a number of Western congressmen and senators who wanted no Federal interference with their propagandization of the advantages, beauties, and opportunities of the West.

As the legislative dust began to rise, requests for copies of *Arid Lands* poured into congressional offices. On March 3, 1879, the House and Senate concurred in a resolution authorizing the printing of 5000 more copies, 1000 for the use of the Senate, 2000 for the use of the House, and 2000 for the use of the Interior Department. Powell now had all the copies he needed, and he distributed them to scientists in various colleges; to agricultural, geographical, geological, and other types of scientific societies; to influential persons devoted to social problems; and to newspapers.

The political and legislative storm soon broke, and it would continue to rage for several years. Powell would be publicly acclaimed as a sage, judicious, and brilliant scientist who not only had great understanding of Western problems but possessed the ability to solve them with wise and practical programs that would benefit the economy of the entire nation. He would be viciously condemned, especially in the Western press, as a visionary, a charlatan, and a revolutionary. He would be hailed as a genius, and branded a dunce. He would be accused of plotting to undermine and destroy progress in the development of Western resources, and he would be praised as a man of unassailable integrity, who was striving to preserve the valuable heritage west of the 100th meridian, so much of which already had been stolen from the American people by the machinations of unconscionable politicians and dishonorable private interests.

When at last the pressures upon him had become

41

more than he could bear, when the onslaughts had become greater than he could hope to combat, he would withdraw from the field, not in disorderly flight but with cold dignity.

John Wesley Powell's *Arid Lands* report, had it been heeded, would have supplanted waste and exploitation and graft with scientific, honest, practicable, and just development of a region that embraced 40 per cent of the area of the United States.

In a few pages he swept aside the fallacies and misconceptions that the American people harbored about the West. He replaced fantasy with reality. With incontrovertible facts he made apparent the assininity of such slogans as "rain follows the plow," which promoters had persuaded misguided, ignorant, hopeful settlers was the gospel truth. He made it clear that "rugged individualism," which Americans had been taught to cherish as a constitutional, if not a divine, right, was anything but an asset to persons living in the West. He demonstrated that by attempting to be independent, to stand on his own feet, a farmer in the region of little rainfall could hardly escape adversities that would ruin him. *Arid Lands* proferred a plan that would have brought prosperity and stability where economic and social chaos reigned. It presented the means whereby countless thousands of families could have been protected from poverty, hunger, and defeat.

Wagons moving east—east, not west—from the high plains, filled with bony half-starved men, women, and children, and painted with the tragic words IN GOD WE TRUSTED, IN THE WEST WE BUSTED, would not have been a commonplace sight—that is, if Powell's words had been heeded, always a necessary qualification in speaking of anything he tried to do. It must be kept in mind when one states that the laws he advocated, the programs he proposed, would have

5]

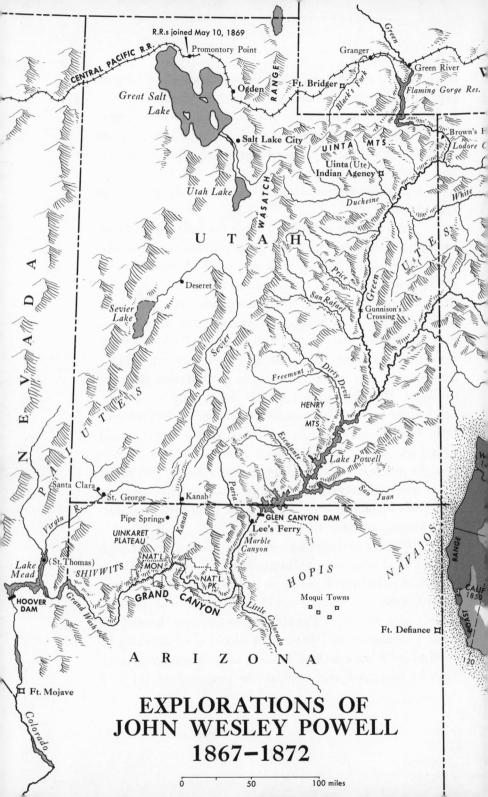

EXPLORATIONS OF
JOHN WESLEY POWELL
1867–1872

0   50   100 miles

Upper map labels:

North Platte

N E B.

W O M I N G
R O C K Y
Laramie • Cheyenne •
UNION PACIFIC R.R.

South Platte

NORTH PARK
FRONT
MIDDLE PARK
Hot Sulphur Spgs.
Empire • • Denver
RANGE
SOUTH PARK
▲ PIKE'S PEAK

GREAT
PLAINS

KAN.

C O L O R A D O

M O U N T A I N S

Grand (Colorado)

Gunnison

Arkansas

Lower map labels:

110   100   90   70

ME.
MONT.
1889
N.D.
1889
VT.
N.H.
IDAHO
1890
MINN.
1858
N.Y.
MASS.
CONN.
R.I.
Ft. Hall •
S.D.
1889
St. Paul •
WIS.
80   70
EAT
WYO.
1890
GREAT
MICH.
Chicago •
PA.
NJ
Cheyenne •
IOWA
1846
Joliet •
Salt Lake City •
NEB.
1867
Omaha
Council
Bluffs
OHIO
W.VA.
VA.
Washington, D.C.
UTAH
1896
Denver •
COLO.
1876
Normal •
ILL.
IND.
KY.
Colorado
MO.
1821
SIN
KAN.
1861
C. Girardeau •
Cairo •
Nashville •
TENN.
N.C.
GRAND
CANYON
N.M.
1912
OKLA.
1907
ARK.
1836
Shiloh •
S.C.
ARIZ.
1912
MISS.
ALA.
GA.
80
TEXAS
1845
Mississippi
Natchez •
LA.
1812
FLA.
New Orleans
110   100   90

VERAGE ANNUAL RAINFALL
- ▓ 20 inches or more
- ▒ 10–20 inches
- ☐ Less than 10

tes show when western states admitted

prevented the great water wars between Western states—wars such as that between Kansas and Nebraska and between the states of the Colorado River Basin, which clogged the courts for years, cost the taxpayers millions of dollars, and engendered bitterness and animosities that stifled progress. Powell called for uniform laws that would have prevented such controversies. He wanted to make water rights inseparable from land rights. His theory was simple: to be workable and support a family, a small piece of land in the arid West must have an assured supply of water for irrigation. Monopolies of water supplies, such as those held by big cattlemen, should be prevented. Where water was available in sufficient quantities, irrigation projects should be built. The smallest grazing ranch that could be profitable must contain from four to six sections of range.

There would have been no disastrous dust bowls if Powell's recommendations had been carried out. There would have been no vast areas forever made useless by erosion. Watersheds would not have been destroyed, with the result that great floods carried away irreplaceable soil and created havoc and disaster in regions that might have contained bountiful farms and prosperous towns. The great high plains that supported uncountable millions of wild animals would not have been destroyed, for Powell would have prevented homesteading and farming in areas—and these contained millions of acres—to which water could not be supplied but which in their natural state were superb grazing lands for cattle and sheep.

John Wesley Powell was not heeded. Congress surrendered to the forces of commercial mendacity and greed, to Western land promoters, cattlemen, water monopolies, and railroads, and to politicians from all sections of the country who found that by rejecting his bills they could gain votes for their own pork-barrel projects.

John Wesley Powell was repulsed. *Arid Lands* was sent back down Capitol Hill and into limbo. Its grave might have been marked only by a file number had not a few determined and sincere men persisted in keeping it alive, a few scientists and members of Congress dedicated to continuing Powell's crusade to drive the spoilers from the West, to conserve the West's wealth, until its resources could be developed in a manner that would not only benefit its people but bring the West to its rightful place in the American economy and social order.

Arid Lands lived, although its heartbeats were only faintly heard through the political walls around it, and the voices of those exalting it were scarcely audible in the noisy protests against all Federal controls which were raised by swindlers; timber, land, and water thieves; and Western state governments.

The last two decades of the nineteenth century had passed before American thinking became influenced to an appreciable extent by the understanding that the principles set forth in *Arid Lands* were just and sound and that the programs it advocated were both wise and feasible. Yet, it was not too late to follow a number of the courses Powell had charted. Some of the goals he had set still could be attained.

Progress was excruciatingly slow. Politicians in the pay of cattlemen's associations, land and water combines, and rabid states' rights proponents continued their attempts to pigeonhole all new Western development bills in Congress. Nevertheless, in the face of this powerful opposition, a number of the plans presented in *Arid Lands* were carried out, some of the laws it proposed were enacted, and some of the reforms it recommended were adopted.

But it was too late to follow the Powell blueprint in full. That could never be done, for too many irremediable mistakes had been made, too many legal snarls had been created, too much of the Western land was held in deed by private interests that should never have been permitted to get their hands on it, too much of the precious natural resources had been stolen, too much of the West had been forever destroyed.

The twentieth century had begun, and John Wesley Powell was an old man, before Americans understood that he had been a brilliant prophet and that what he had foreseen so many years before had happened.

II

WHEN POWELL MADE HIS FIRST TRIP TO THE Rocky Mountains, in the summer of 1867, the era of Western geographical discovery had ended. There were a few "blanks" on Land Office and War Department charts, but these, with one notable exception, were comparatively small. Not all the West between the eastern Great Plains and the Cascades in California had been adequately mapped—far from it—but most of this vast region had been traversed and examined to the extent that its waters, ranges, altitudes, and sharply contrasting climates could be delineated and recorded with fair accuracy. The single truly large unexplored area contained the lower Green and upper Colorado Rivers. For the most part several hundred miles in width from east to west, it reached for almost 1000 miles, as these wild streams ran, from northern Utah to far western Arizona, below the Grand Canyon.

The frontier, in the generally applied sense of the

11]

word, was gone in 1867. Actually, there had not been for a decade—and longer in some sections—a border marking the end of settlement and the beginning of wilderness. Towns, mining camps, military stations, trading posts, and agricultural and ranching communities existed, although often at wide intervals, from the Missouri to the Pacific. Stage lines connected most of them. Completion of the first transcontinental railroad was only two years in the future. The plundering of Western lands, water supplies, and timber and mineral resources already had reached almost inconceivable proportions, and the wanton wastefulness was being permitted to continue with virtually no effort on the part of the Federal government to halt it. The Homestead Act, signed in 1862 by Abraham Lincoln in the sincere but mistaken belief that it would give every poor man a chance to obtain free a farm of 160 acres, had swiftly shown itself to be unworkable west of the 98th meridian. Not only deficiencies in the statute defeated the good intentions with which it had been written. Speculators, aided and abetted by crooked Land Office officials and underpaid clerks, were able to circumvent its provisions and get control of millions of acres for paltry under-the-counter payments. Mining and lumber combines were being "sold"—really negotiated thefts—mineral and timber lands worth hundreds, and often thousands, of times the prices paid for them. Railroad companies were by far the largest landowners in the West. Millions of acres were arbitrarily withdrawn from homestead entry—in some places in strips forty to eighty miles wide along a proposed route— and given to the railroad companies to encourage construction.

John Wesley Powell was thirty-three years of age in 1867, a maimed man who might understandably have pursued his career as a teacher, as his preacher father strongly urged him to do, and have enjoyed security for the remainder of his active years. The idea was abhorrent to him. He could not abide for a moment the thought of spending his life lecturing to the sons and daughters of farmers and small town merchants, almost all of whom could be depended upon to return directly from college to their homes, forget natural history and geology, and devote themselves to having babies, tilling fields, and working behind the counters of queensware stores.

From the time of his boyhood, when he had labored from dawn to dusk on a frontier farm, Powell's intellect, ambitions, and dreams had transcended the ordinary and restricted courses open to most persons born to his social level and the privations and backwoods environment he knew. He craved knowledge, not just any kind of knowledge, not simply information, but learning supported by proved facts that might be effectively applied as an instrument to force open closed doors.

As a youth he had been attracted by natural phenomena. A freshwater clam, a woodland plant, a ledge of rock, the contours of hills against the Midwestern sky, had fascinated him, and he had known no peace until he had identified them, discovered the forces that had created and shaped them, and awarded them their proper places in the evolution of the earth. If, however, his innate tendencies had given him direction, early experiences and the education he acquired had stirred in him a devotion to science that was indestructible and had set him upon a road that he understood had no ending, for always there would be new mysteries to be solved. It was a road from which he would never deviate.

Powell, the bearded, stocky, one-armed professor of natural history from a small Illinois college, brought to the

West a new type of scientific mind. He had been preceded by a number of distinguished botanists, zoologists, ornithologists, geologists, geographers, and cartographers—Bradbury, Schoolcraft, Nuttall, Maximilian of Wied-Neuwied, James, King, to name a few—but none of them had harbored his intentions, ambitions, hopes, or plans. They had gone out to see and to record, to examine and gather specimens, to establish boundaries and draw maps, and almost invariably their work concluded with the success or failure of these specific missions. That was not true of Powell. His accomplishments in the West, his technical studies and reports, were foundations upon which he hoped to construct far greater projects. They were intended to serve as stepping-stones to the fulfillment of his dreams.

For Powell's thinking, even in his early days as a teacher and a curator, went far beyond the ordinary spheres of scientific endeavor. It went into the world of human life, spanning from the Paleolithic to the new mechanical age in which he lived, and which he saw rapidly moving toward undreamed-of heights. It went from the geologic levels beneath the surface to the pulsatile realm in which mankind was born, struggled, and disintegrated to dust. It went from raw nature to sophisticated politics, from primal ooze to modern culture.

To Powell, acquired knowledge had very little value unless it was used as the basis for constructive action. Knowledge was ammunition to be fired at ignorance, apathy, waste, and corruption. It was building material to be used in erecting bulwarks that would protect and conserve resources, not for the few but for all mankind. It was light to be spread from sea to sea to drive away the blanket of darkness which robber barons and selfish captains of industry had drawn over Americans and in which they sought to imprison them.

Powell represented not only a new type of scientist but a new breed of politician. As courageous and daring and dedicated as his predecessors, he possessed attributes they had lacked: the objectivity of the intelligent and rational reformer; the determination to reshape legal, social, and political institutions that had grown out of misconceptions and dishonest motives; the unquenchable desire to enlighten Americans with methods, organizations, projects, and programs that would benefit not only the individual but the country. He had the faculty of attracting colleagues of similar understanding and hope. He was the founder, organizer, and guiding genius of a small coterie of brilliant men of vision who succeeded in awakening Americans to the dire need for just, efficient, and socially beneficial development of the West.

But in 1867 John Wesley Powell was far from being a celebrity. Indeed, outside central Illinois his name was scarcely known. He had taught for a short time at Illinois Wesleyan University, a struggling Methodist college in Bloomington. His salary was $1000 a year—not a lavish sum—but the position offered him an opportunity to devote himself to natural science. For his pay he lectured on botany, cellular histology, comparative anatomy, physiology, zoology, insects injurious to vegetation, natural philosophy, geology, and mineralogy.

Bigger and better fields, if not less arduous duties, were nearby. In the adjoining town of Normal were located both the Illinois State Normal University and the heterogeneous collections of the Illinois State Natural History Society. Powell had been one of the founders of the society and for a time had served without remuneration as its secretary. He arranged to move to Normal as a professor of geology —but without disclosing his extensive plans.

Powell's inherent skill as a promoter, his adroitness as a negotiator, and his ability as a politician soon made themselves apparent. They would never in his long career, even on the highest levels in Washington, be better demonstrated than they were at this time.

When the State Legislature had granted a charter to the State Natural History Society, it had failed to provide either funds for a curator or to defray expenses of caring and housing the collections. Professors, including Powell, had contributed as much of their time as possible in efforts to achieve some sort of order in the steadily growing contributions. But the Historical Society Museum, located in a University building, remained a disorderly repository that could be likened to a dusty attic.

Powell casually, but not without studied persistence, talked to University administrators of the value of the collections, pointing out that an orderly and efficiently managed natural history museum would be an asset of which no other college in the state could boast. His quiet campaign brought results. If there was anything, besides more money, that Normal desired, or needed, they were prestige and public recognition. In November, 1866, Powell was sent to Springfield to ask the Legislature for an annual appropriation to support the museum.

Powell's pleas to committees and individual legislators were finished performances. His military service, during which he had commanded large numbers of troops, had taught him much about manipulating and swaying men. His enthusiasm was contagious, his calmness and confidence persuasive, his arguments thoughtfully designed to appeal to political minds. The people of a great new state like Illinois should not be denied advantages and an opportunity to absorb knowledge that were accorded to the citizens of the world's most progressive nations—England, Scotland, Belgium, France, Sweden, Russia—and enlightened Eastern states—New York, Virginia, Massachusetts—all of which maintained similar museums with public money. The Smithsonian Institution in Washington received an annual Federal appropriation.

If it was not to be hoped that in the foreseeable future the little museum in Normal might rival these large and heavily endowed institutions, the legislators chose to overlook that consideration. In February, 1867, the Illinois House and Senate passed by unanimous vote the bill Powell had written and proffered. Its structure left no provision for controversy.

In order that the [State Historical] Society may carry out its purpose, it should have a general commissioner and curator, who can give his whole time to the work of the society; and whose duty it would be to superintend the researches and collections, take charge of the museum, carry on the exchanges, and make the distributions.

The aggregate of this expenditure would be about twenty-five hundred dollars; fifteen hundred dollars for the salary of the general commissioner and curator; and one thousand dollars for books, apparatus, etc.

There was no doubt as to who wanted the appointment. Powell made that clear in a series of private audiences and confidential letters. The State Board of Education set March 26 as the date on which a special meeting would be held in Normal to consider the matter, but before that time Powell had been assured he would be named curator and had been asked to prepare a brief acceptance speech. The vote in his favor was unanimous.

Powell's acceptance speech amounted to little more than "Thank you. I am honored. . . ." He then proceeded

17]

to disclose a plan that had been taking shape in his mind for some weeks. The interests of the museum could not be better served than by the acquisition of new collections from distant fields. The natural history of Illinois was already amply portrayed. To provide the museum with comprehensive and valuable displays that would open new and greater opportunities to college students, specimens should be obtained from other regions. The Colorado Rockies would be a good place to begin. As a matter of fact, he had been hoping to make a trip west during the coming summer, taking with him a number of students and teachers who could afford to pay their own way.

There would, of course, be inescapable overall costs to be borne. Equipment, horses, scientific instruments, and experienced helpers had to be obtained. He had ideas as to how these expenses might be defrayed, but it would be most agreeable if at least part of the $1000 appropriated by the Legislature "for books, apparatus, etc."—say $500—might be used for this purpose. The entranced board voted unanimously for the allocation.

The $500 was helpful but far from enough. With his own money, Powell promptly bought a train ticket to Washington, D.C. There he made two important calls. The first was at the office of his old commander, General Grant, who was serving as Secretary of War *ad interim*. Grant issued an order to Army Commissary depots in the West to supply the Powell expedition with rations at cost. Another order signed by Grant directed the commander of the Department of the Platte [Nebraska and adjoining territories] to furnish Powell's company with a military escort through the dangerous area northeast of Fort Laramie.

His next Washington stop was the Smithsonian Institution. Its Secretary, Dr. Joseph Henry, who would become one of his greatest friends and supporters, readily agreed to loan him numerous scientific instruments in exchange for topographic measurements made in the Western mountains and plains.

Armed with the War Department and Smithsonian endorsements, en route home Powell visited the offices of several railroads and express companies with the suggestion that it might be good public relations for them to provide free transportation for himself, his men, and their baggage. He arrived back in Normal with passes valued at more than $1700 and agreements under which the expedition's equipment and boxes of specimens would be carried to their destinations free of charge.

Powell turned next to institutions he believed would be interested in becoming associated with his expedition for the purpose of obtaining collections duplicating those he would send to the State Museum. The response was not as favorable as he had hoped it would be. However, from Illinois Industrial University (to become the University of Illinois) came $500 and from the Chicago Academy of Sciences he received $100 and a quantity of tools.

The complement of the expedition consisted of three college seniors, seven amateur naturalists, and the curator of the State Museum at Normal, whose qualifications as a professional might have prompted misgivings in high scientific circles. One of the amateurs was Powell's wife, Emma, who was listed as an ornithologist. Whatever she lacked in training and experience was offset by a strong constitution, enthusiasm for the trip, steady nerves, and not a little talent as a camp cook. She had demonstrated her ability to withstand the rigorous life in the open and had displayed not the slightest squeamishness while participating in anatomical dissections of birds, beasts, and reptiles.

Most cautious and practical scientists, except John Wesley Powell, would have hesitated to undertake an expedition to the Rocky Mountains under the conditions he faced. He had $1100 in cash contributions in his wallet. His personal financial condition was precarious. The house he had purchased in Normal was heavily mortgaged. He had a few hundred dollars in his bank account. His income was $1500 a year. There were no indications that additional funds might be forthcoming from any source. If debts were incurred, he alone would be responsible for them.

Yet he did not hesitate to continue preparations for the journey, and Emma made no effort to stop him. She shared his attitude and his confidence. She knew, as well, that any attempt on her part to dissuade him not only would be useless but might result in his going without her. She understood him, fully aware of his craving for action and consuming desire to penetrate at least a small part of the vast unknown realms of the Western wilderness.

In the last week of May, Powell and Emma reached Council Bluffs, Iowa. The other members of the expedition were on their way west. They were:

Entomologists: A. H. Thompson, Bloomington; Reverend William E. Spencer, Rock Island, Ill.

Botanist: T. J. Burrill, Urbana, Ill.

Zoologists: Reverend J. C. Hartzell, Bloomington; F. M. Bishop, Marquette, Mich.

Ornithologists: E. W. Spencer, Rock Island; S. H. Huse, Evanston, Ill.

Herpetologist: M. Titterington, Rock Island.

Mineralogist: S. H. Kerrick, Bloomington.

Artist: George D. Platte, Rock Island.

Grant's order opened for Powell the door to the quarters of General William Tecumseh Sherman, commander of the region. When he heard Powell's plan to travel to Colorado by way of the Dakota badlands and Fort Laramie, Sherman shook his head. It would be a dangerous route. There was every reason to believe that the summer of 1867 would bring fighting as bloody as that of the past two years. Tribes of the northern plains, especially the Sioux, were on the warpath. The building of the Union Pacific and the increasing pressures of white settlement had infuriated them, and they had already made savage raids that had taken a heavy toll of military and civilian lives. If the intelligence he had received could be believed, the worst was yet to come. Sherman advised Powell—actually ordered him— to travel by way of the Platte to Colorado, a more southerly route than he had chosen but one that would provide some protection by established army installations.

Undoubtedly Sherman would have been grateful if Powell had taken his little band of greenhorns back to the museum in Normal, but it was not within his province to bring about that desirable situation. He issued an order for Army scouts to accompany the expedition from post to post and directed his quartermaster to comply with Powell's requests for rations, clothing, and equipment—at cost.

On June 1, two heavily loaded wagons and a group of mounted novices moved slowly out along the worn trail that ran along the south bank of the Platte. Barometers, telescopes, nets, traps, and specimen boxes far outnumbered the weapons they carried. It must have been a somewhat ludicrous and discouraging sight to the lean burned men in buckskin riding in the lead, whose keen eyes swept the endless rolling sea of plain ahead, not in a search for bugs and birds and peculiar bits of rock but for some sign that would warn them of the dangers they knew very well might be encountered.

What Powell himself did on the 1867 trip to Colorado and what he and his colleagues accomplished in the way of scientific studies are matters of small consequence. What is important is that the expedition marked the beginning of a career unique in American history and on it were borne forces that, in time, would shatter universal conceptions and traditions.

Early in July, Denver was reached without misfortune. Powell, never averse to publicity he believed might be beneficial, made a point of meeting William N. Byers, editor of the *Rocky Mountain News* and Colorado historian. Byers introduced him to other prominent persons (scientists were still curiosities in the booming mining capital) and to experienced mountain men who could give him good advice if not personal assistance. Stories of the expedition in the *Rocky Mountain News* and the *Daily Colorado Tribune* brought Powell several invitations to speak, which he gladly accepted.

During the summer the Front Range was traversed in various places, Middle and South Parks were visited, Pikes Peak and Lincoln Peak were climbed, a whole month was spent in the delightful valley known as Bergen's Park, and some of the canyons of the Grand River, headwaters of the Colorado, were explored. Wagonloads of specimens were collected; innumerable bales, boxes, and sacks full of skins, plants, insects, birds, rocks, and ore samples were sent to Denver for shipment to Normal. Packsacks were heavy with books containing meteorological and topographical observations, diaries, and scientific notes.

All the members had started home by September 1, but Powell and Emma continued their exploring and collecting until snow drove them out of the mountains. Traveling by stage and train, they reached Normal in mid-November.

If anything, the Illinois State Historical Society Museum, which he had promised to make the biggest and best of its kind in the Midwest, was in greater confusion than when he had left it in April. Adding to the disorder were great piles of specimens gathered in the plains and mountains.

Powell went dutifully to work, welcoming the aid of any student, faculty member, or friend who was able to contribute even brief time to sorting and classifying and arranging the conglomerate exhibits. "We confess our surprise," said a story in the *Bloomington Daily Pantagraph,* "at the amount of material collected. Too much credit cannot be given Professor Powell. He works sixteen hours a day and pays four assistants out of his own meager salary."

Professor Powell was working long hours, but during many of them his thoughts were on matters far removed from the problems of the museum. Long before the winter had passed he knew what he would do when spring came, and the cold days seemed to him to drag along with aggravating slowness.

III

JOSEPH POWELL WAS A FARMER, A TAIlor, and a Methodist exhorter. Instead of making him a man capable of earning a living in several ways, this curious combination of vocations created conflicts in him that gave rise to a certain instability. In his early twenties, competent with a needle as well as a hoe, he had sought to escape the hard labor in the fields of his native Shrewsbury by seeking work as a journeyman tailor in London. Inordinately devout even as a youth, he devoted himself as much as possible while sewing seams in a London sweatshop to studying for the ministry. Inadequate education and a lack of time away from making a bare living put ordination as a minister beyond achievement, but eventually he was licensed "to exercise his gifts in the Methodist Episcopal Church so long as his doctrines, practice, and usefulness comport with the discipline of said church."

In the course of his religious work he met Mary

Dean, a young woman from Hull who had similar ambitions to dedicate herself to God's service. The pulpit being closed to her, she was preparing herself for missionary work. Evangelical zeal and love, both, perhaps, equally profound in each of them, drew them together. Joseph's desire to emigrate to America and preach to heathens in the wilderness was in accord with Mary's hope to aid in carrying the gospel to foreign shores. In 1828 they were married, but the arrival of two daughters in the next two years, and the necessity of acquiring enough money for the journey, prevented them from sailing until 1830.

Hearing that a number of English and Welsh families had settled in Utica, New York, they chose it as their destination. The English and Welsh families were there, but Utica also had six churches of various denominations, and no resident seemed to be without an opportunity to receive religious instruction. Also, there was a surplus of tailors, and other types of employment were scarce.

Joseph Powell managed to acquire a horse and cart, and he and Mary, who was again pregnant, and their two infant daughters set out for Palmyra, where he had heard that an opportunity to preach and work could be found. The information turned out to be erroneous. Palmyra and the adjacent countryside were being occupied in steadily increasing numbers by members of a new sect who called themselves Latter-Day Saints. Their leader, Joseph Smith, claimed to have found gold tablets bearing words indecipherable to everyone but himself. Gifted with divine powers, he had been able to translate the cryptographic messages and had included them in a bulky volume, *The Book of Mormon*.

Joseph Powell looked upon Smith as a false prophet and prepared to push on. Somewhere along that rutted road lieved it would, this persuasion enhanced his own qualifications for a place in heaven, it denied due credit to an earthly giant named George Crookham.

Crookham, who stood well over six feet and weighed more than 300 pounds, was a Pennsylvanian who had moved westward to southern Ohio at the turn of the century, on the heels of the retreating Indians. He had been highly successful as a farmer and stock raiser and was one of the largest landowners in the area. Although he had received no formal education, he was exceptionally well read, and he possessed a library containing scores of volumes of history and literature, a number of them in Latin, which he read and spoke with proficiency. Although books were a great source of pleasure to him, his greatest loves were natural history and science. He had constructed a spacious study and museum on his farm homestead. In it he housed the artifacts he had gathered over nearly half a century, Indian relics, preserved plants, insects and reptiles, mounted birds and animals, a collection of scientific works, geological specimens, and apparatus for conducting various experiments with ores, soils, and chemicals.

The door of the Crookham museum stood open to anyone seriously interested in acquiring knowledge. He read to illiterate farmers, lectured, and conducted classes on various subjects, at no cost whatsoever to his pupils, almost all of whom were mature men and women. Shortly before Joseph Powell had the good fortune to meet him, Crookham had placed the management of his farms and properties in the hands of his sons and was devoting himself to the study of natural sciences and to writing local history.

The friendship of George Crookham and Joseph Powell was based on more than a personal liking for each other. Crookham was an ardent and vocal abolitionist, and